Y0-EMJ-566

DANIEL BOONE

DANIEL BOONE

WRITTEN BY ESTHER AVERILL

ILLUSTRATIONS BY FEODOR ROJANKOVSKY

HARPER & BROTHERS · NEW YORK AND LONDON

CONTENTS

THE HUNTER

HIS is the story of the hero of the Wilderness. He was a hunter, and his name was Daniel Boone. Boone was not born in the Wilderness; no white man had yet been born there. Few white men had seen it. Daniel Boone was born east of the Wilderness, on the frontier of Pennsylvania, in 1734. This was on the border where the world of the white men ended and the Indian world began.

7

Sometimes, in the night, along the border, Indians swooped down and scalped the settlers.

But the Indians who came to the settlement where the young Daniel lived were friendly. They brought the furs of animals that they had hunted and they traded these furs for colored beads and rifles.

Daniel learned the forest secrets of the Indians. The Indians walked so silently that not a twig cracked underfoot. They knew the trails and habits of the animals and could imitate the cries of animals and birds.

When Daniel was old enough, he wore a little deerskin suit, Indian moccasins and a coonskin cap. Then he pretended that

he was a mighty hunter, and just as soon as he could hold a rifle, learned to shoot.

He learned to shoot so well that he built a hut in the forest. There he spent long days hunting — and exploring.

8

He loved the forest; loved its silences and shapes and colors. He loved its dangers, too. This, Daniel decided, was a man's world. He was still just a boy himself, but he did a man's work in hunting. He hunted bear and deer and provided the family with meat.

When Daniel was sixteen, his father moved the family south in search of better land. They hitched the horses to the wagon. On the wagon rode Daniel's mother with the younger children and the girls, the pots and pans, the farm tools and the precious spinning wheel. The men folk formed an escort, walking with rifles on their arms, for fear of hostile Indians.

The caravan moved slowly.

The horses could go fast enough, the men folk could walk fast enough. But there was trouble with the cows. The Boones had brought cows, and the cows walked behind the wagon, sometimes very far behind it. They liked Pennsylvania and were in no hurry to move on.

Pioneers like Daniel's family had patience. The caravan made progress—slow progress, but it was progress. The countryside began to have a wild, strange look. Sometimes it seemed to Daniel's mother that they were going to the western Wilderness. But they continued to go south and finally, after several hundred miles, reached North Carolina and settled in the valley of the Yadkin River.

There they did as they had done in Pennsylvania. They cut down trees, made a clearing in the woods and built a cabin of logs. They plowed the land and planted Indian corn and sweet potatoes. And Daniel went hunting and provided the family with meat.

BOONE GREW TO BE THE GREATEST HUNTER IN THE HISTORY OF AMERICA

THE
EXPLORER

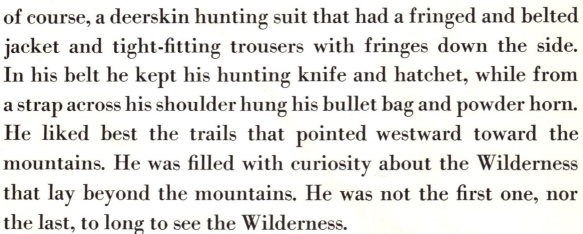

DANIEL stood five feet, ten inches in his moccasins and wore, of course, a deerskin hunting suit that had a fringed and belted jacket and tight-fitting trousers with fringes down the side. In his belt he kept his hunting knife and hatchet, while from a strap across his shoulder hung his bullet bag and powder horn. He liked best the trails that pointed westward toward the mountains. He was filled with curiosity about the Wilderness that lay beyond the mountains. He was not the first one, nor the last, to long to see the Wilderness.

But when he was twenty-one, a war broke out against the French and Indians. So he went northward and not westward, and became a wagoner in the army that had been sent from England, under General Braddock, to protect the Colonies. By the campfire at night Daniel talked with a trader, named John

Finley, who had actually been in the Wilderness beyond the mountains. Finley told of its gigantic forests and of the herds of buffaloes that thundered through its valleys. As Daniel listened, he longed more than ever to explore the Wilderness.

But after the Braddock expedition, Daniel married and built his own log cabin in North Carolina. Afterward there was a new baby in the cabin nearly every year.

Daniel farmed and hunted and carried deerskins to the nearest trading post to exchange them for the things the children needed.

When James, his oldest boy, was eight, Daniel took him into the forest and began to teach him to hunt.

Rifles in those days were very long, and before each shot a hunter had to ram a bullet down the barrel with a long, fine rod—a ramrod. The best distance for a perfect shot was about a hundred yards. So the hunter crept silently to his prey and aimed. He froze himself like a tree or rock and waited. Then, when the animal turned around or raised its head, *zing!* went the bullet and hit the animal between the eyes.

James learned to shoot and to follow trails of animals. He liked best, of course, the trails that pointed westward toward the mountains, and he loved to listen to the stories that his father told of the Wilderness beyond the mountains. They were mostly stories that had been told by the trader, Finley, in the Braddock expedition.

Daniel had not given up his dream of going to the Wilderness.

But the Wilderness was barred and hidden by a wall of mountains, from the warm lands in the south as far north as Canada. In North Carolina, where Daniel lived, were many mountain ranges, one behind the other. They became his favorite haunt. He went there, usually alone, on long trips of exploration. Gradually, among the mountains, he discovered old trails made by the wild animals and Indians. He himself made new trails through the mountain gaps.

And so he climbed from range to range and finally succeeded in reaching that part of the great Wilderness which became Tennessee.

But the part he wanted most of all to see was the more northern part—Kentucky.

1769

THE KENTUCKY WILDERNESS

ONE day the trader, Finley, who had been a wagoner with Daniel in the French and Indian War, drifted into North Carolina, to the settlement where Daniel lived. What happened next was bound to happen. Finley and Daniel Boone made up their minds to go together to the Kentucky Wilderness. Four other men decided to go, too, and Squire Boone, who was Daniel's younger brother, said that he would follow in the autumn when the crops were in.

The six men began their journey in the spring of 1769. Their route lay northward and then westward through the mountain ranges of Virginia. They went on horseback, carrying very little but their beaver traps and extra ammunition.

It took the men four weeks to cross the first two mountain ranges. In the fifth week they rode along an Indian warpath and went through a gap, called Cumberland Gap, which was in the third and last range. Below them, to the west, as far as the eye could see, stretched the Kentucky Wilderness. It was a green Wilderness. The more Boone saw of it, the more he felt that it was Paradise.

On the hills and in the valleys roamed tremendous herds of buffaloes. Deer and smaller game abounded, and in the swamps were black bears trying to escape the summer heat.

The meadows were carpeted with soft grasses and sweet-smelling clover. On the river banks were fields of cane; its stalks were often five times taller than a man. But most amazing were the forests. They were a wonder to behold.

There were forests everywhere, forests of giant hardwood trees —the sycamore, the tulip tree, the oak and the chestnut. These trees grew very tall and very straight. Some of them were ten feet in diameter. Their wide-spreading branches met far overhead and shut out all the sunlight. From the branches hung wild grapevines that were strong enough to hold a man.

Boone climbed them and learned to swing himself up into the branches of the trees. This was a handy thing to know, in case hostile Indians came. No Indians came. The forest remained silent, except for the cries of animals and birds.

FOUR MEN DISAPPEAR

THE six men found a sheltered spot beside a river. There they built a camp of boughs and skins, and all through the summer months they hunted deer and piled the deerskins in the camp. Deerskins, when sold at home, would pay for the expenses of the expedition.

Fear of hostile Indians kept the men together. But now and then Boone slipped away to admire the Wilderness.

Everything in the Wilderness was big. Sometimes, when Boone was in a meadow, the sky above was darkened suddenly by great clouds of birds. Those birds were passenger pigeons, and on some days millions of them flew overhead.

19

In fields of cockleburs and in the groves of sycamores were bright green birds, called parakeets, that hung from branches like small acrobats and often completely covered a tall tree. In summer, the color and abundance in the Wilderness made Boone think that he was in a southern land.

But when winter came, the Wilderness became a harsh, cold, northern land. One had to have a kind of fire inside oneself to keep alive.

Snow lay everywhere, and the deer went into the hills to seek food in secret places. So the hunters became trappers, and broke through the icy rivers, laid down their beaver traps and piled the beaver skins beside the deerskins in the camp.

One day Boone and another man, John Stuart, went to hunt buffaloes in the canebrake. Suddenly, out of the tall, dense cane arose a band of Indians who surrounded Boone and Stuart, captured them and took them northward to the Indian camp. At night the prisoners slept between two guards.

One night Boone raised himself on his elbow and discovered that the guards were half asleep. The crackling of a twig would have aroused them. But Boone crept away without a sound, and Stuart followed. They reached the forest and escaped.

But when they reached their camp, they found it plundered. Indians had been there. The deerskins and the beaver skins were gone.

Finley and the three other white men were gone also.

No one ever found out what had happened.

ALONE IN

THE GREAT

WILDERNESS

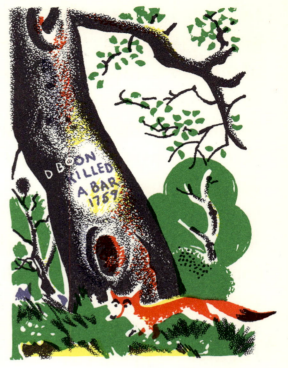

STUART was the next to disappear.

Boone and Stuart had moved their camp to a more secret place where no Indians could find them. But Squire Boone found them. This favorite, younger brother, Squire, had said that he would follow when his crops were in. So he had followed through five hundred miles of Wilderness and snow, arriving on horseback with another man, John Neely. There were now four white men in the Wilderness. But one day Stuart vanished. Five years later Boone found the bones and powder horn of Stuart in the hollow of a great sycamore tree. No one ever really knew what happened.

Meanwhile, John Neely grew alarmed. He was a brave man, but the Wilderness was too much for him. He took his skins, got on his pack horse and rode home, alone.

Daniel and Squire Boone remained together in the Wilderness. They trapped and hunted, and in the spring Squire took the deerskins and the beaver skins to North Carolina to sell. He promised Daniel that he would return in the autumn.

Daniel could have gone home, too. But it was spring in the Kentucky Wilderness. The deer were in the forest. The green parakeets were in the cockleburs and sycamores. In the fields were dogtooth violets, bluebells and pink lady's-slippers. The laurel was in bloom. All the Wilderness was his—his to explore —if the Indians would let him.

Boone ranged the forests. He carved the record of his hunting feats on trees, and gazed in wonder at the giant bones of animals that lay around the salt springs. The race of giant animals had disappeared, but the salt springs (or licks) remained. Deer and buffaloes now came to lick salt from the earth around the springs.

For months Boone remained alone in the great Wilderness without a horse, a dog or any living soul to talk with. But he was happy—so happy that sometimes he lay on the ground and sang at the top of his voice.

But he did not sing when Indians were near. Then he kept very still, or hid in caves. And he was always careful of his footprints. Often he covered them with leaves. Often he walked through the streams or swung from grapevines and left no prints at all. One day, however, Indians crept up behind him. He was standing on a high precipice, looking at a river which was more than sixty feet below him. The Indians, who had been pursuing him, were sure they had him. But he leaped suddenly from

the precipice, landed in a treetop, slid down the tree, swam the river and escaped.

Squire Boone came back into the Wilderness, found Daniel and went home again. Then Squire came back a third time and went home finally with Daniel. They carried a great pile of skins. But near the mountains the two brothers were attacked and robbed by Indians. Daniel, therefore, after two years of absence, returned home empty-handed. But he had seen what he had wanted most of all to see—the Kentucky Wilderness.

He knew that he would not be satisfied until he went back there to live.

WHAT DID YOU SEE THERE, DAN'L?

HIS neighbors asked him, "What did you see there, Dan'l? Come, Dan'l, tell us what you saw out there beyond the mountains."

Sometimes Boone replied, "A second Paradise."

But this was not the kind of answer he could give to many people.

Usually Boone talked about the great abundance of wild animals and the richness of Kentucky soil. So, if a man went there with his family to live, all that he would need would be a rifle, a bag of corn to plant, and a sharp ax to clear the land and build his cabin.

The neighbors listened eagerly. From tongue to tongue, along the border, sped news of the Kentucky Wilderness and of the land and freedom that it offered.

THE DEATH OF JAMES

TWO years after his return from Kentucky, Boone was ready to go back there with his family. His wife and younger children got on horseback with the bags of corn, the farm tools and the spinning wheel.

James, the oldest boy who was fifteen, walked with his father to protect the family from hostile Indians.

The younger children were in a state of great excitement. They had often played that they were living in the Wilderness. But this would be the real thing, and in a few weeks they would swing from wild grapevines and peer into mysterious Kentucky caves.

Suddenly the children remembered the story of a bear that their father once had told them.

It had happened in the Wilderness, when Boone was living there alone. One day he left his hat upon the ground, and while his back was turned, a black bear shambled up, stole the hat and hurried off with it. Boone chased the bear, shot it and rescued his hat.

So now the children called to their older brother, James.

"James," they cried, "if a black bear comes in the great Wilderness and steals our coonskin caps, will you shoot the bear?"

"Why, certainly," said James, "I'll shoot the bear."

Six other pioneer families, with their children, cows and pigs, joined the Boone family on the way. All of them planned to settle in the Wilderness, together.

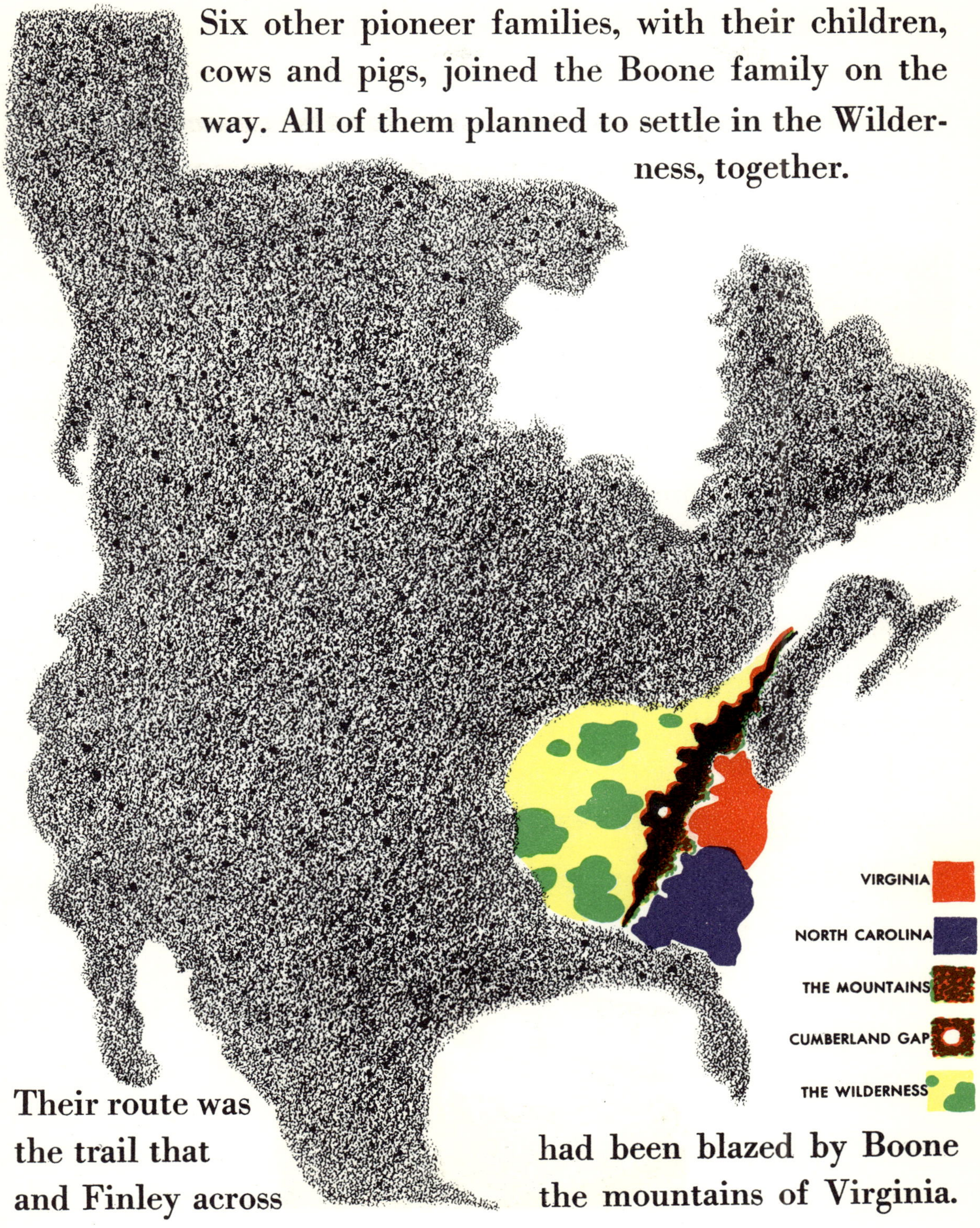

Their route was
the trail that
and Finley across
had been blazed by Boone
the mountains of Virginia.

VIRGINIA

NORTH CAROLINA

THE MOUNTAINS

CUMBERLAND GAP

THE WILDERNESS

Forty armed men had promised to escort the pioneers across the mountains to Kentucky. The pioneers made a camp at the foot of the mountains and waited for the armed men.

James, meanwhile, was sent ahead to see a man named Russell about additional supplies. James saw Russell and was returning to the camp with several other men when darkness overtook them. They decided to remain in the forest for the night. But in the dawn, while they were sleeping, they were attacked and murdered by a band of Indians. Daniel found James lying in cold blood.

The death of James went very deep with Daniel. James was his first child and eldest son. When James was just a little boy, his father had taken him into the forest to teach him to hunt. Several times they had spent months together in the forest. Sometimes Boone had tucked the small boy inside his own big hunting shirt to keep him warm.

So James never saw the Wilderness. The blow that killed him was the first of many blows the Indians struck, that year, against the white men.

AMERICA'S MOST FAMOUS SCOUT

ALL the land of North America had been the hunting ground of the Indians before the white men came. And then the white men came from Europe, settled on the hunting grounds between the sea and the mountains, and drove the Indians westward beyond the mountains, toward the setting sun.

Now the white men wanted to go westward, too, and take the Indian hunting grounds beyond the mountains. The Indians were angry and bewildered. They daubed themselves with war

31

paint and they watched and waited, ready to attack all pioneers who tried to cross the mountains.

Boone decided that it was too dangerous a moment to attempt to settle with his wife and children in the Wilderness. He found a cabin for them in Virginia, while on the border the Indians were swooping down and raiding settlements.

At this time, in the Wilderness beyond the mountains—somewhere—was a group of white men who had gone to begin the work of measuring the land and marking boundaries. These surveyors must be warned that trouble with the Indians had reached a breaking point. The most famous scout in all America was sent to find them. This scout was Daniel Boone.

Boone went on foot, accompanied by another scout. In sixty days they traveled eight hundred miles, found the surveyors and guided them to safety.

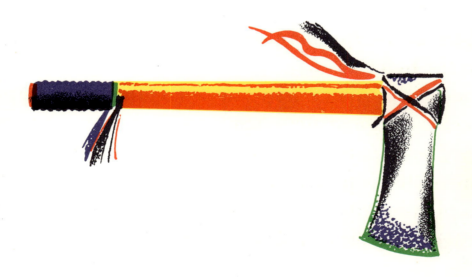

THE WILDERNESS ROAD

WAR against the Indians was declared in the following spring. It was the spring of 1774, and Boone was made a captain in command of all the forts along the border. The war is always called Lord Dunmore's War, because Lord Dunmore was the Governor of Virginia and he raised the troops that fought the Indians. The Indians were defeated in the autumn.

Then Boone began to make new plans for going to the Kentucky Wilderness to live. The feeling, too, had grown in him that he should open the Wilderness for all white men who wanted land and freedom.

He once told a friend, "Many dark and sleepless nights have I been a companion for owls, separated from the cheerful society of men, scorched by the summer's heat and pinched by the winter's cold—an instrument ordained to settle the Wilderness."

As for the Indians, no tribes really lived in Kentucky. Shawnee Indians lived north of it and Cherokee Indians lived south of it. Both tribes, however, used Kentucky as their hunting ground. Of the two tribes, the Cherokees were believed to have the stronger claim to it.

So Boone arranged for the Cherokees to meet a business man, named Henderson, at a place called the Sycamore Shoals, which was beyond the border. Henderson, who was rich, was interested in buying Kentucky from the Cherokees. He hoped of course, to make a profit by reselling it to settlers.

Twelve hundred Cherokee warriors, squaws and children came to see the price that Henderson would pay. The price was fifty thousand dollars' worth of white men's goods. It was not much to pay for a great Wilderness, but all the goods looked very tempting when spread beneath the trees, for there were colored shirts, earrings, firearms and other things that Indians loved dearly.

A pipe of peace was smoked, papers were signed, and the Wilderness was sold.

A chief, named Dragging Canoe, then said to Boone, "Brother, we have given you a fine land, but there is a dark cloud hanging over it. I believe you will have much trouble settling that land."

Boone went right ahead. With thirty men he cleared the old trails to Kentucky and cut new ones through the canebrake and the brush. These trails, when joined, made one long road into the Wilderness. It was called the Wilderness Road, and it ended on the banks of the Kentucky River.

On the banks of the Kentucky River, Boone and his men began to build a settlement which consisted of a few log cabins and a fort. Henderson came not long afterward with other men

and helped to complete the building of the settlement, which was called Boonesborough.

In the autumn Boone went to Virginia and returned with his wife and children. Other families arrived before the winter. During all this time the Indians caused no trouble. But in December two boys went into the forest and were attacked by Shawnees from the north. One boy was killed; his body was discovered. Of the other boy, no trace was ever found.

THE CAPTURE OF JEMIMA BOONE

FAR, far away across the mountains, in the east, the Colonies were fighting England for their independence. But news of those great battles, which would decide the destiny of America, was slow to penetrate the Wilderness. The real world of the settlers at Boonesborough was the Wilderness itself—and the little fort that sheltered them.

The fort, which stood a short distance from the river, was shaped like a rectangle two hundred and fifty feet long by one hundred and seventy-five feet wide. Its walls, which were twelve feet high, were made of heavy logs set upright in the earth and pointed on the top.

In each corner, where the walls met, was a blockhouse to be used in time of battle. And in the walls themselves were thirty cabins where the settlers lived. A few other cabins were outside the fort, closer to the river. Boone, with his wife and children, lived in one of these.

The first winter in the Wilderness was a long, cold winter, and everyone was glad when spring came finally and the crops, that had been planted in the autumn, poked their green shoots through the soil.

For a long time there had been no sign of hostile Indians. So one Sunday afternoon in June, Jemima Boone, who was Daniel's oldest daughter, went to the river with two girls of her own age. Jemima was fifteen. They took a bark canoe (the Indian kind) and just for fun they paddled up the river. As they drew near the opposite shore, five Indians rose from the canebrake, seized the girls and ran away with them.

The kidnapping of the girls was not suspected until late in the afternoon when it was time for them to milk the cows. Then the men of Boonesborough went to the river and found the empty bark canoe, as well as Indian footprints. The footprints vanished in the canebrake.

In a ravine beyond the canebrake were tiny signs left by the girls themselves. Scared as they had been, they had managed now and then to break a twig or drag their feet in mud.

Boone said that from his knowledge of Indians he guessed the kidnappers had escaped along the hilltops and would take the Warrior's Trace (a war-path) north to the Shawnee villages.

Unfortunately, the Indians had been traveling for several hours, and night was falling. Boone and his men were obliged to wait until dawn to pick up the trail. But at the crack of dawn they found the trail and followed it for thirty miles. Then Boone cut straight across the country. It was a gamble, but it was his only chance to overtake the kidnappers.

Now in the rescue party were three young men who were the sweethearts of the girls, and they kept pace with Boone. So the party sped along and on the second morning, reached the Warrior's Trace.

There were Indian footprints on the Trace. Evidently the kidnappers no longer dreamed of being overtaken. Farther on was a dead buffalo. It had just been killed and blood was running from its hump. Boone said he guessed the Indians were cooking lunch.

He found them in a clearing in the forest. A hump of buffalo was roasting on the fire, and tied to a tree were the three captive girls. Boone and his men were hidden in a thicket. They had made no sound, but they had taken aim. Boone gave the signal. *Zing!* went the bullets. Two Indians were killed and three ran off. The girls were saved.

Not long afterward there were three weddings in the Wilderness. The three girls married the young sweethearts who had helped to rescue them.

So the story of the kidnapping, because of the romance and because of the bravery of the girls, brought tears into the eyes of many of the Kentucky settlers.

The Indians, however, were interested in the brains behind the rescue. Those were the brains of Daniel Boone. Boone was

the person whom the Indians longed to capture. Often they had tried to capture him, and always they had failed. But the Indians were patient. They would bide their time.

39

THE CAPTURE OF DANIEL BOONE

BOONE was captured finally in a blinding snowstorm. He had gone on horseback to the Blue Licks to get salt for the settlers who were in desperate need of it. Forty men accompanied him. Fires were built and great iron kettles were filled with the salt water from the springs. Then began the slow, tedious work of boiling away the water until only the salt remained. It required many days.

Sometimes, while the water boiled in the great kettles, Boone would take his horse and go off hunting.

THESE ARE FOOTPRINTS OF ANIMALS IN THE SNOW

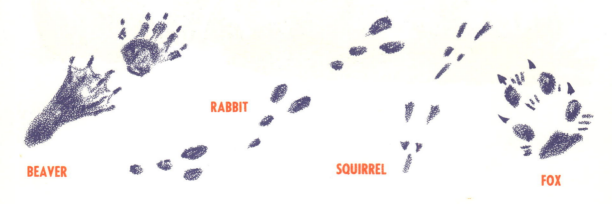

BEAVER   RABBIT   SQUIRREL   FOX

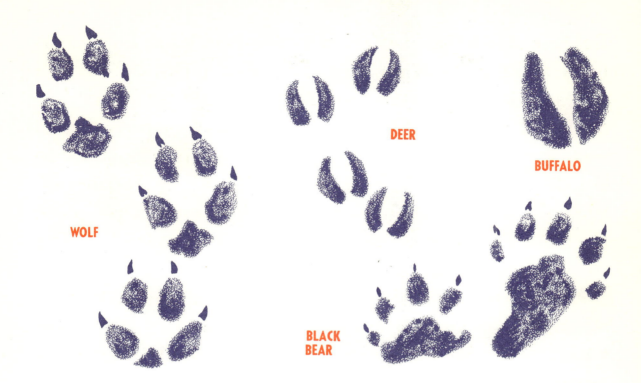

WOLF

DEER

BUFFALO

BLACK
BEAR

One day he went to hunt buffaloes. It was a bitterly cold day. The snow was deep, and now and then it slipped with a crash from the branch of an enormous tree.

Boone shot a buffalo, sliced the meat and tied it on his horse. As he trudged back toward the Blue Licks, the snow began to fall again. It fell so fast that Boone could scarcely see a yard ahead of him. Suddenly Indians surrounded him. They were so numerous that he could not escape.

The Indians led him to their chief, who was the great Blackfish. Blackfish was in a near-by clearing of the forest with his warriors. There were hundreds of them. All of them were daubed with gaudy war paint, for they were on the warpath.

They were on their way to attack Boonesborough!

Boone realized that the fate of all the families at Boonesborough, and the fate of the men at the Blue Licks, and his own fate, too, depended on the next few minutes.

So first of all, to save himself, he tried a ruse. He pretended to be weary of the hard life of a settler. He said that he would be delighted to become an Indian. His words were translated for Chief Blackfish by a Negro boy, named Pompey, who had joined the tribe. The Chief was pleased that Daniel Boone was willing to become an Indian. Boone's life was spared.

Boone's next step was to try to save the families at Boonesborough from an Indian attack. He lied again and told the Chief, "If you will wait until the spring, I shall bring all my people to live with you in your village. But wait until the spring. It is too cold to take the women and the children now." Chief Blackfish consulted with his warriors and decided to wait. Then Blackfish asked Boone where his comrades were.

"I will guide you to them," Boone replied, "if you will promise not to kill or torture them."

Chief Blackfish promised, and Boone led the Indians to the Blue Licks. There, by means of signs, he told his comrades that the wisest course would be for them to surrender. They surrendered and were treated well.

How proud the Indians were of their white prisoners! How especially proud they were of Daniel Boone! The prisoners were marched north to Chillicothe, the village of the Indians, and were exhibited in triumph before the tribe.

HOW BOONE ESCAPED

ALTHOUGH he was an enemy, the Indians liked Boone because in many ways he was an Indian. He fought, he hunted and he used his knowledge of the woods as well as the best Indians.

Besides all this, Boone joked at danger and he had a magic trick. His trick was to take a hunting knife and swallow it and then, to everyone's amazement, draw it from his hunting shirt.

So Chief Blackfish decided to adopt Daniel Boone to take the place of a real son who had been killed by white men. The ceremony of adoption, which was supposed to change Boone from a white man into an Indian, was performed this way:

43

First, all the hair was plucked from Boone's head, except for a patch on his crown. This patch served as his scalp lock and was braided and beaded.

Then his body was painted with Shawnee symbols, and he was given beaded ornaments for his neck, his arms and wrists. And Blackfish made a speech.

Afterward the squaws took Boone and bathed him in the river. They scrubbed him hard until they believed that all his white blood had been washed away.

Next he was led into the council house. All the warriors were there, and he was given several bright red feathers for his scalp lock and a pipe to smoke. Blackfish made another speech, and the ceremony ended with a feast of venison and corn.

So Daniel Boone became the adopted son of Blackfish, and a member of the Shawnee nation.

Boone's Indian name was Sheltowee, which means Big Turtle.

There was a real friendship between Chief Blackfish and his white son, Big Turtle. Only, Big Turtle did not wish to be an Indian son. He wanted to return to his wife and children whom he had left at Boonesborough.

Four months passed and during that time Boone lived the kind of life he loved. He hunted, trapped and breathed the free air of the forests. But day and night he watched for an opportunity to escape.

The Indians, in their turn, watched Boone constantly. Much as they trusted him, they were not absolutely sure that he wanted to remain with them.

One day the whole tribe went hunting in the forest. Boone, however, stayed with the squaws and children in a clearing. He chatted quietly with the squaw who was his mother by adoption. Then he noticed that the men were aiming at a flock of wild turkeys that had been driven in- to a tree. The eyes of  every Indian were on those turkeys.

Boone walked calmly to his horse. He cut away the pots and kettles that were strapped to it and jumped on horseback. Off he galloped.

The squaws and children screamed. The men came running. But Daniel Boone had vanished.

The Indian men picked up his trail and tried to overtake him. His trail vanished, too.

Meanwhile, Boone rode down a stream that left no trace that could be followed. And when night came, he rode on land. And when day came, he left his weary horse and ran on foot. He covered up his footprints in every way that he could think of. Sometimes his pursuers found his trail, but lost it quickly.

Boone ran on and on, and finally he reached the banks of the Ohio River. The river was in full flood. But at his very feet, as if God had put it there, was an old and battered bark canoe. It had a hole in it. Boone patched the hole and paddled to the opposite shore.

Four days after his escape he reached the banks of the Kentucky River. Ahead of him was Boonesborough. But his cabin was deserted. His wife and children, believing him dead, had gone back east, beyond the mountains.

Other families, wearied of the dangers and the hardships of the Wilderness, had gone, too. Only thirty men, twenty boys, a few women and a few children remained at Boonesborough.

But Boone's cat was there. She had been left behind. She came slowly from the woods and looked at him. Then she rubbed against his legs, climbed upon his knee, sniffed his sleeves, his chin and chest, and smelled the smell of Indians. She wondered why her master had been gone so many moons.

1 7 7 8

THE BATTLE OF BOONESBOROUGH

BOONE did not go east immediately to get his wife and children, whom he longed to see. Instead, he remained at Boonesborough and prepared the fort for battle.

Blackfish came in September with four hundred and forty Indian warriors in vermilion war paint. But Blackfish wanted to give Boone a chance to avoid a battle by surrendering the fort and going to live at Chillicothe among the Indians.

So the Indians lifted a white flag of truce and Boone walked out of the fort to speak with Blackfish.

"My son, why did you run away?" asked Blackfish sadly.

"I wanted so much to see my squaw and children," Boone replied.

"If you had only told me," Blackfish said, "I would have let you come. I would have helped you. Come with me now, without a battle, for I can take your people, too. See, I have brought forty horses. They will carry your old men, your women and your children."

"The trail is long," said Boone. "The matter must be discussed in council. I shall give you my answer tomorrow."

Boone was marking time. Thirty white men, twenty boys, and a scattering of women and children were not enough to defend Boonesborough against four hundred and forty of the enemy. He had sent to some of the new settlements in Kentucky for assistance. He waited all next day, but reinforcements did not come. In the evening Boone went out to Blackfish. Blackfish was still hopeful.

But Boone said, "We shall defend the fort while there is a man alive."

And so began the first great battle in the Wilderness.

The Indians fired their rifles from the surrounding forest and from the hills across the river.

One of the enemy climbed a tree close to the fort and sniped.

He killed several of the animals that were in the fort and finally hit Jemima Boone in the shoulder. (Jemima was Daniel's married daughter). Then Boone leaped on top of a blockhouse, aimed his long rifle, fired and with one shot brought a dead man from the tree.

The fort, of course, had no roof, and all the cows and pigs, the horses and the oxen, the ducks and chickens, and the cats and dogs of Boonesborough had been brought into the enclosure for the duration of the battle.

Back and forth among the animals ran the women and the children, who molded bullets, helped to load rifles, and carried food and water to the riflemen.

Day and night the twenty riflemen stayed at their firing posts and managed to hold off the Indians. Most of the firing was done from loopholes in the walls.

Usually an Indian attack lasted only one day, or two days at the most. But this attack went on and on. It lasted three days— four days—and the end was not in sight. The settlers had run out of food and water. They were exhausted from the lack of sleep.

On the fifth day, the Indians began to shoot flaming arrows at the fort. Some of the logs caught fire, but there was not a drop of water to keep the fire from spreading. A boy leaped up and beat out the flames with his hands.

On the sixth day, the fort took fire again. On the seventh day, while the fort was blazing, the sky suddenly grew dark and

with a roll of thunder, the
sky opened and a torrential
rain poured down
and quenched the
flames.

Ever since the beginning of the siege, the Indians had been trying to dig a tunnel to the fort. The Indians did not like to dig; they thought it was a squaw's work. But they had with them some military advisors who had been obtained from among the French and the English. The military advisors urged the Indians to continue digging. And as the prize was Daniel Boone, the Indians dug.

On the eighth day, when they had almost reached the fort, the earth, which had been soaked by continuous rain, gave way. The tunnel caved in. The Indians lost heart and gave up the siege. Yet as they went northward to their village, Blackfish still had hopes that the great fighter, Daniel Boone, would come some day to Chillicothe and join the Indians.

THE BATTLE OF THE BLUE LICKS

THE last big battle in the Wilderness was fought at the Blue Licks. Blackfish was dead—he had died fighting against the white men. But other Indian chiefs were on the warpath, and they came in the summer of 1782 with three hundred warriors and raided one of the new settlements that had sprung up in Kentucky.

Two hundred white men, all on horseback, rushed to the assistance of the settlement. Daniel Boone was with them. So was his son, Israel. The Indians retreated to the Blue Licks, and the white men followed.

At the Blue Licks was a river, and beyond the river stood a hill. Indians could be seen along the hilltop, but in such tiny numbers that Boone's suspicions were aroused. Indians usually fought their battles under cover, and he believed that these few Indians were a decoy to lure the white men on. He advised against an immediate attack.

But all the younger men were eager for a fight. So the white troops rode across the river, dismounted and charged on foot toward the hill. Boone commanded the left wing.

Suddenly, *aou! aou! aou!*

Hundreds of yelling Indians rose over the hill, descended on the troops and pushed them back to the river. One third of all the white men were killed outright, and many more lay wounded.

Boone was the last to leave the field. His son, Israel, had just fallen; blood was gushing from the boy's mouth. Boone picked him up and carried him. The boy died in his father's arms.

A huge Indian, with lifted tomahawk, bore down on Boone. Boone dropped the body of his son and raised his rifle, shot the Indian and escaped.

The Battle of the Blue Licks lasted fifteen minutes. It was a great military victory for the Indians. They went home to celebrate what seemed to them to be the doom of all the white men in the Wilderness.

But in the autumn, one thousand white men, including Daniel Boone, carried the war northward into the Indians' own country and burned the Indian crops and burned the Indian villages. Chillicothe, where Daniel Boone had been a captive, was utterly destroyed.

The Indians did not recover. Now and then they went on the warpath and, of course, a white man's scalp was never safe. But the long and bitter years, the years known afterward as the "dark and bloody years," were over.

The Wilderness was won.

NEW HUNTING GROUNDS

"IF I DIE," said Boone, "wash my body, lay it straight, wrap it in a clean blanket. Bury me on the hilltop . . . mark the trees so that my family and friends can find my grave . . . take my rifle home."

He was quite old by then, and had fallen ill while hunting in Missouri. But he recovered and good years were still ahead of him—years of hunting beyond the Mississippi River.

Daniel Boone had left Kentucky. This is what had happened: After the battle of the Blue Licks, after the Kentucky Wilderness was won, settlers poured in by the tens of thousands and the Wilderness began to vanish. Among the settlers were fine pioneers and splendid hunters. But greedy men came, too. These greedy men snatched land that belonged rightfully to other people, and they snatched the land of Daniel Boone.

Boone believed the land he lived on belonged rightfully to him because he had been the first to settle on it. Besides, he was the person who had opened the Wilderness, led the white men in and fought in all their battles. But he had been too occupied to write his claims to land on legal paper. So, when his land was taken, he could not get it back.

The loss of his land left Boone penniless and in debt. He put his family and a few possessions on a flatboat and headed westward down the Ohio to the Mississippi River.

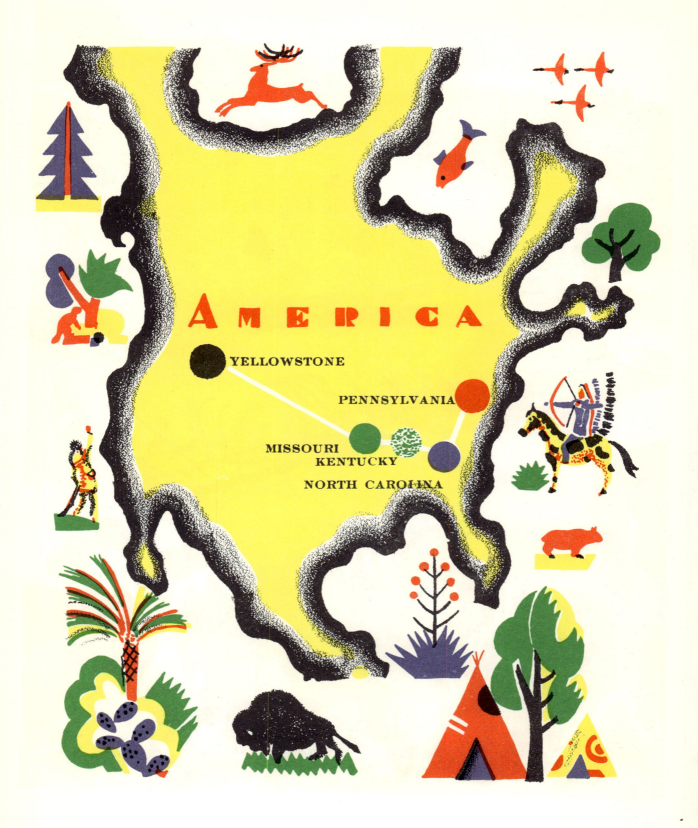

AMERICA

YELLOWSTONE

PENNSYLVANIA

MISSOURI
KENTUCKY
NORTH CAROLINA

The Spaniards in Missouri gave him land that was surrounded by great forests, filled with game. Boone, however, did not spend all his time hunting. He spent many winters trapping beaver. Finally, with the money from the sale of beaver skins, he made a short trip to Kentucky and paid back everything he owed. He had half a dollar in his deerskin shirt when he went home. But he was happy. He had paid his debts. Now he could go hunting.

His clear blue eyes still led him on from forest trail to forest trail. He died in 1820, at the age of eighty-six.

Before he died he went hunting as far west as the Yellowstone.

There, in the untouched forests and great open spaces,
he found once more the bears, the deer, the
herds of buffaloes and all the other animals of that early Wilderness
which had seemed like
Paradise.